# Here I Am
## Concord Connections

David Maguire

Published by emerson books


Design and Graphics by

Cindy Murphy, Bluemoon Graphics


ISBN-13: 978-1979517331

ISBN-10: 1979517339

Library of Congress Control Number: PENDING

CreateSpace Independent Publishing Platform, North Charleston, SC

LCCN Imprint Name: emerson books, Concord, Massachusetts

# Contents

# Dedication

This book is dedicated to all the great Concordians who have helped to shape American history and our culture.

# Preface #1

# Impressive Young Man with an Inspiring Story

By Rick Frese

What inspires us most are people who overcome adversity and go on to pursue their dreams. David Maguire is an impressive young man with an inspiring story to share. In *Here I Am*, a creative tribute to his hometown, he has captured the character, spirit and historic underpinnings of Concord, Massachusetts.

During the spring semester 2015, I was honored to receive an invitation to speak at Lasell College, David's alma mater. Following the presentation, the college's president hosted a social gathering, which provided an opportunity for me to mention David Maguire's name, a fellow Concordian whom I knew to be a Lasell alumnus. Beyond just remembering David, the college administrators spoke admiringly of his courage and determination to achieve academic excellence.

Having grown up in a house on land once owned by the Alcott family, David is proud to be part of an authentic American town, the first inland settlement in the colonies. Known as the site of the first Revolutionary War battle, as well as home to the literary giants of the 19th Century, Concord is steeped in history dating back to 1635.

David's unique personalized guide to prominent historic sites and renowned Concord luminaries is highlighted by rich anecdotes. He either informs or reminds the reader, that Thoreau was born David Henry Thoreau, subsequently preferring his middle name, or that Wright's Tavern in the center of town was the meeting place for the colonial Provincial Congress on April 18th 1775, the night before the skirmish at the North Bridge. Following the skirmish, British military leaders briefly established headquarters there, becoming then a temporary home to friend and foe alike.

Jack Maguire reports that David cherishes the wisdom of Dr. Seuss's *The Lorax*. Well, paraphrasing another quote from Seuss, "Unless someone like you cares a whole awful lot"... effectively, nothing is accomplished.

David Maguire *cares a whole awful lot.*

Rick Frese, longtime Concordian and university professor, is author of *Concord and the Civil War: From Walden Pond to the Gettysburg Front.*

# Preface #2

# A Celebration: Two Concord Davids Stand Alone

By Jack Maguire

Historic Concord has been my family's hallowed home for almost forty years. My two heroes named David were both born here in Concord. The following poem, "The Creation of David," is dedicated to my son David Maguire and to his namesake, David Henry Thoreau:

## The Creation of David

A quirky quantum trace
Froths from its timeless sea,
Inflating, creating space.
The Cosmos is free!

Waves of radiation flash
Across the swelling sphere,
As energetic photons clash,
And massive quarks appear.

When protons and electrons form
As ions in a plasma ball,
Neutrinos penetrate and swarm
And cooling atoms finally fall.

At once the universe expands
And gravity becomes the force
To execute Einstein's commands—
The stellar and galactic source

In time the supernovas fuse
Carbon, iron, stuff of life,
Until more cataclysms choose
Planets, moons and Darwin's strife.

Our Earth is only one blue dot
A haven in this cosmic storm
Where once the dinosaurs were taught
That here a firestorm could form.

Are Egypt's pharaohs still in power?
Did Ozymandias survive?
Have tyrants thwarted freedom's flower?
Can truth and love and beauty thrive?

Ten billion years have now gone by;
Man muses on his earthly throne,
Reflecting on the wondrous sky—
While loving David stands alone.


David Maguire was born with cerebral palsy and language disabilities. His parents were told by his doctors that he would likely never walk, talk, or attend regular schools. But David's indomitable spirit resulted in the miracle of a four-year college degree and the character of one of the finest, kindest young men I have ever known.

It should be clear in interpreting this humble poem that David's proud dad is more a scientist than a poet. The poem traces a Scientist/Transcendentalist's view of how our universe, planet, and mankind evolved from the Big Bang to our precarious present state as we celebrate Thoreau's 200th birthday.

Here is where David Henry Thoreau (only after graduating from Harvard in his 20s did Thoreau arbitrarily transpose his name to Henry David) enters the poem's picture:

- **Thoreau the Scientist** was one of the earliest strong supporters of "Darwin's strife," the theory of evolution. Thoreau had read with enthusiasm Charles Darwin's *On the Origin of Species* and challenged other prominent scholars of his day who doubted evolution. Today Thoreau would be at the forefront of those endorsing natural selection as a fundamental principle of science.

- **Thoreau the Naturalist** would have continued to be our champion of conservation. He studied the subtle changes over time in the habitats of flora and fauna at Walden Pond, in Walden Woods, and all along the Concord River. Henry would have been a dedicated defender of Planet Earth — Carl Sagan's Pale Blue Dot — against the ravages of over-industrialization and human-induced global warming.

- **Thoreau the Freedom-Fighting Pacifist**, memorialized on the Great Stone Circle in Walden Woods by Mohandas Gandhi, Emily Dickinson, and Martin Luther King, would today still be an advocate of Percy B. Shelley's stand against tyranny and slavery in his powerful sonnet, "Ozymandias."

> "… Nothing beside remains. Round the decay
> Of that colossal Wreck, boundless and bare
> The lone and level sands stretch far away."

Henry would have responded passionately to two of the poem's questions, especially foreboding today: Did Ozymandias survive? And have tyrants thwarted freedom's flower?

- **Thoreau the Transcendentalist, philosopher** — lover of wisdom — partnered with fellow Concordians Emerson, the Alcotts, Margaret Fuller, and Hawthorne — among our greatest Americans — in affirmatively answering the poem's profound question, "Can truth and love and beauty thrive?"

The primary inspiration of "The Creation of David" has been my son David. Thoreau's fellow Concordian exemplifies David Henry's ideals in the heroic, yet humble way he lives his life of challenges.

David cherishes the wisdom of Dr. Seuss's *The Lorax*, also carved in stone in Walden Woods: "Unless someone like you cares a whole awful lot, nothing's going to get better; it's not."

Hence a most fitting ending to "The Creation of David": *Loving David stands alone.*


Jack Maguire is David's father, a citizen of Concord and a member of Thoreau Farm's Board of Trustees.

# Introduction

*Photo of Concord's North Bridge, taken by David Maguire*

# Introduction

I was raised in Concord, Massachusetts. Concord is one of the most important towns in the whole world — a place where the American Revolution began with the "shot heard round the world," a place where some of America's most famous authors (Louisa May Alcott and Nathaniel Hawthorne) lived and wrote, and a place where the thinking of great American philosophers like Ralph Waldo Emerson and Henry David Thoreau influenced the world. I was brought up in a home built on land once owned by the Alcotts, and I attended Alcott School.

With the help of family, friends and Lasell College faculty, I have studied and written about Concord's interesting history. I have inserted myself directly into that history through photographs of famous monuments, homes, buildings, and gravesites. I have benefitted from the knowledge of many people who have taken me on tours, shared their writings, and told me stories about my family connections to American history, and especially to Concord.

I have also toured important monuments in Washington, D.C., in order to connect great men of American history (Thomas Jefferson and Abraham Lincoln) with the events in my hometown of Concord. While I spend time in this book talking about the important sites (in Concord and Washington, D.C.) themselves, my real goal is to make CONNECTIONS wherever possible — connections of the American Revolution and the terrible tragedy of slavery to Concord's literary history, and connections of Concord's proud history to my own family.

# Part I:

## April 19, 1775
## The First Day of the Revolution

# Wright's Tavern

Here I am standing in front of Wright's Tavern, which was where the British made their first stop in Concord on April 19, 1775. The British soldiers went into the tavern to try to find out where the Minutemen had hidden their guns and ammunition. They suspected that they used the tavern as a meeting place to plot rising up against England. Something I found interesting about the tavern's history is that a committee of the Colonialists' Provincial Congress met in Wright's Tavern the night before the Revolution broke out. Then, the night after the first day of the Revolutionary War, the British military leaders met there.

But why was Wright's Tavern so involved in the first days of the war? I think the tavern is a logical place for political meetings because of its close connection to the community. Taverns were hangouts for men where they drank ale and talked about their lives. I can imagine that many of these conversations turned to heated discussions about whether or not the Colonialists should seek independence. Community talk became more passionate and people began to organize around their ideas. This is just a theory, but I can see how loud discussions over drinks may have become quiet meetings about how to seek independence.

# First Parish Church, Concord

Here I am standing in front of the historic First Parish Church, which was the site of the first Continental Congress, run by John Hancock in 1774. The first pastor was Peter Bulkeley, who was a blood relative of the Emersons. In this situation, the religious lives of the people were mixed with political hopes and dreams. To this day, the First Parish Church, which I attend, is very active in important current events. Members of the church support poor communities in other parts of the world, welcome refugees into Concord families until they can get their lives started in America, and sponsor speakers for a wide range of political opinions, which include quotes from Muslim, Hindu, Buddhist, Jewish, Catholic, and atheist leaders. This church is next door to Wright's Tavern, where political meetings and debates once took place.

# Harvard University in Concord During the Revolutionary War

Here I am facing Wright's Tavern. Right across the street from Wright's Tavern on the road from Lexington to Concord is the building where Harvard University was located during the Revolution. The University moved out to Concord to avoid all the bullets in Cambridge. This small building held the classrooms, the dormitory, and the library. After the war, Harvard moved back to Cambridge, and many years later two of Concord's most distinguished citizens, Ralph Waldo Emerson and Henry David Thoreau, attended Harvard University. My grandfather, Wallace Cox, attended Harvard University at the same time as President John F. Kennedy.

# The Concord Fight

Here I am next to the plaque called "Concord Fight" that describes the battle at the Old North Bridge on April 19, 1775. This is an interesting plaque to me because the way it is written makes it possible for me to imagine exactly what the battle looked like and how it happened. It even has quotes from men as they readied to fight. You can feel their excitement and their fear. This is understandable since they were men who had just come in from their farms with little or no training — and they were standing up against one of the best equipped and trained armies in the world. Their bravery is incredible to me. When they saw smoke coming from their town, they must have thought that the British were burning down their homes. This is a great example of what men will do to protect their families and the land they love. The same is true today as I watch people with no weapons standing up against armies with military might.

# Concord: Old North Bridge and Minuteman Statue
# April 2010 Flood Begins

The greatest flood in the last one hundred years hit Concord in early April 2010. Here is the Old North Bridge with the Minuteman guard on the far side. The water from the flood is so high that we can begin to see the trickle heading toward the bridge itself. Because the town and the federal government care a lot about Concord's and America's history, the Bridge has been taken care of over the years despite having once been washed away and replaced. If this hadn't been done, the bridge would have been washed away for good. The bridge is a symbol of America's fight for freedom against all odds. The bridge was the divider of the Minutemen and the British soldiers. They stared at each other from each side of the bridge for what must have seemed like a really long time before the first shots were fired.

# Old North Bridge:
# April 2010 Flood Continues

Here I am on April 2, 2010, standing in water which has come over the Bridge with the Concord Minuteman over my right shoulder in the background. When America celebrated its 200th anniversary, the Bicentennial, President Ford came to Concord to celebrate where and how it all began. Luckily, we didn't have a flood that year!

What an amazing coincidence that these photographs were taken in April during a flood at this famous "rude bridge." This also shows the connection between this philosopher/writer's view of the Revolutionary War many years later. His phrase about the "shot heard 'round the world" is famous. He reminds the reader that America's Revolutionary War began in this remote farmland and started revolutionary uprisings around the world. For instance, many historians connect the French Revolution to the American Revolution. That the Colonialists managed to defeat such a powerful country had tremendous impact.

# Old North Bridge: Where British Soldiers Fell

Here I am standing behind the monument to the revolution that was erected in 1836 at the very spot where the British soldiers fell. I think this was a gesture of respect for the British. When my father showed this monument to a Ukrainian exchange student who was living with our family, he told him that two British soldiers had died on this spot. He asked him, "Do you mean two million?" My dad said, "No, two people." He exclaimed, "I can't believe it! In my country, we never put up a monument unless at least a million die!" The Ukrainian's comment made me realize how much we value each human life in our country. Many of the philosophers and writers who taught us to respect the well being of people, animals, plants, and our environment lived in Concord, and may have influenced how our culture thinks about the value of life. Over my left shoulder is the flooded bridge itself with the famous Minuteman Statue on the other side.

# Concord Minuteman Statue

Here is the Concord Minuteman surrounded by water. The gold inscription is a poem written by Ralph Waldo Emerson. It is very ironic that Emerson's words are as follows:

> "By the rude bridge that arched the flood,
> Their flag to April's breeze unfurled.
> Here once the embattled farmers stood
> And fired the shot heard 'round the world."

# Daniel Chester French's Minuteman: The Massachusetts Quarter

Here I am next to a front view of the Minuteman Statue sculpted by Daniel Chester French to commemorate 100 years after the American Revolution. Daniel French was a young man when he created this statue. Amazing! The statue was placed at the Old North Bridge ten years after the worst war ever fought by Americans — the Civil War. It reminds everyone what we fought for in the 1700s, when we wanted our freedom from the British rule. The farmer holding his plow, a symbol of his livelihood, is also holding a gun. He is willing to fight and die for his land and his right to live free. This statue was so famous it was selected to represent Massachusetts on the state quarter.

# Old North Bridge:
# The Two Monuments

Here I am next to the two monuments on either side of the Old North Bridge. The British stood on this side and the Minutemen stood on the other.

HERE
On the 19 of April
1775
was made
the first forcible resistance
to British aggression
On the opposite Bank
stood the American Militia
Here stood the Invading Army
and on this spot
the first of the Enemy fell
in the War of that Revolution
which gave
Independence
to these United States
In gratitude to GOD
and
in the love of Freedom
this Monument
was erected
AD 1836

# 1836 Monument: Old North Bridge

Here I am next to the inscription on the 1836 monument. Note that it refers to "the first forcible resistance to British aggression." It also refers to the "invading army," and expresses "gratitude to God in the love of freedom." This monument has passionate language that describes the British as the enemy. It reminds me of propaganda to make the other side look bad. The same story told on the "Concord Fight" plaque is much less dramatic and aggressive. When our British friends come to visit us, they always laugh when they read this plaque. I'm glad enough time has gone by that we can take these words less seriously.

# Part II:

## Old Hill Burying Ground

# Old Hill Burying Ground — Concord Center

Here I am at the oldest burial ground in Concord, located on a hill in the Center. Many famous Concordians are buried here, including participants in the fight at the Bridge. This is not the famous Sleepy Hollow Cemetery where many well-known authors are buried, but people whom we have studied in our U.S. History classes. For example, the Merriam family lived in a home on the Battle Road (it is still there today) and this homestead was named "Merriam's Bloody Corner" because of the number of Colonial and British soldiers who died on that spot. John Jack was a slave most of his life. Reverend William Emerson, who is memorialized here (but not actually buried here), was Ralph Waldo Emerson's grandfather and a prominent minister.

## Mason's House

Here I am across the Battle Road from the old cemetery. Over my left shoulder is the oldest stone house in Concord, which was built and occupied by Concord's only mason.

# Reverend William Emerson's Memorial: His Church Below

Here I am next to the memorial of Reverend William Emerson, one of the earliest pastors of the First Parish Church below. His memorial is in a spot overlooking the church where he was pastor during the Revolutionary War.

# Reverend William Emerson's Monument

Here I am at William Emerson's monument with the Catholic Church below. There are many churches in Concord. In the colonial days and up to now, churches were and are important places to form communities. People find satisfaction from their membership with others who share their beliefs and they rely on the friendships they make in their places of worship.

# Part III:

Connections
April 19, 1775, The Revolution
The Literary/Artistic Giants

# The Old Manse:
# The Emersons, the Hawthornes, and Thoreau

Here I am standing in front of the Old Manse. On April 19, 1775, the Old Manse was owned by Reverend William Emerson, who watched the battle unfold at the North Bridge from his home. In the years that followed, this home was occupied by Emerson's grandson, Ralph Waldo Emerson, and by newlyweds Nathaniel and Sophia Hawthorne. The Hawthornes moved into this house right after their wedding and, as a wedding gift, Henry David Thoreau gave them a perennial garden that still blooms today. Because of all these connections, the Old Manse is one of the most important buildings in American history.

# Colonial Inn — 1716 in Concord Center: Owned by Thoreau's Grandfather

Here I am standing in front of the Colonial Inn, which you can see from the chimney was built in 1716 (closer to when Columbus discovered America than to 2017). This inn was owned by Henry David Thoreau's grandfather when the war broke out in April 1775. He stood on his porch and observed the Revolution just as Emerson's grandfather was watching farther down Monument Street at the Old Manse. These are important connections among the political, religious, and literary histories of Concord.

# Daniel Chester French's Grave

Here I am next to the grave of one of the world's most famous sculptors, Daniel Chester French. I spent a long time searching for this grave and found it right near Authors Ridge in Sleepy Hollow Cemetery. French is famous for sculpting the Concord Minuteman when he was in his 20s, and, almost 50 years later, the statue of Lincoln at the Lincoln Memorial in his 70s. The two statues represent important parts of America's beliefs. The Minuteman Statue is mostly French's image of the common farmer standing up for his freedom. The Lincoln Memorial shows the next level of America's evolution, because Lincoln fought for the freedom of slaves. French's statues are so famous that they are represented both on the penny and on the Massachusetts quarter. He also sculpted the statue of John Harvard in Harvard Yard.

# Concord Minuteman — 1875

Here I am standing next to Daniel Chester French's statue, the Concord Minuteman. The foot actually points to the place where you can see Daniel French's name.

# Daniel Chester French's Sculpture of Abraham Lincoln in Washington, D.C.

Here I am in Washington, D.C. in front of French's statue of Abraham Lincoln. Later in this pictorial essay, I will cover slavery further because it existed in Concord. As I mentioned before, Lincoln freed the slaves during the bloodiest war in American history. It is ironic that Concord residents owned slaves while fighting for their own freedom in the Revolutionary War.

# The Jefferson Memorial: Washington, D.C.

Here I am standing in front of the Jefferson Memorial. Jefferson wrote the Declaration of Independence, which states, "We hold these truths to be self-evident: that all men are created equal…"

# Jefferson Statue and Declaration of Independence

Here I am inside the Jefferson Memorial next to the statue of one of America's greatest presidents. On the wall behind us is a complete copy of the Declaration of Independence. One famous line is, "All men are created equal." Women were not considered equals, even to our great statesmen, until more than a century later. Also, like some residents of Concord, Jefferson held slaves even as he championed freedom, a contradiction that eventually led to the Civil War. Jefferson publicly spoke about God, but in his private writings questioned the existence of God. He once wrote to his nephew, "Question even God's existence."

Here I Am: Concord Connections

# Part IV:

## Slavery

# John Jack's Gravestone: Old Hill Burying Ground

Here I am next to John Jack's grave in the Old Burial Ground. John Jack was a slave owned by a Concordian. Just before he died, John Jack bought his own freedom. This is a specific example of how the principles Colonialists fought for did not apply to everyone.

od wills us free, men wills us s
will as God wills Gods will be
Here lies the body of
JOHN JACK,
a native of Africa who d
March 1773 aged about 60
Tho' born in a land of slavery,
He was born free.
Tho' he lived in a land of libe
He lived a slave.
Till by his honest, tho' stolen la
He acquired the source of slave
Which gave him his freedom;
Tho' not long before,
Death the grand tyrant
Gave him his final emancipatio
And set him on a footing with ki

# The Famous Epitaph by Daniel Bliss

Here is John Jack's incredible gravestone epitaph. Written by a Tory, Daniel Bliss, the epitaph speaks to the contradictions in the American Revolution, which ultimately resulted in the Civil War.

God wills us free; Man wills us slaves.
I will as God wills, God's will be done.

Here lies the body of
JOHN JACK
A native of Africa who died
March 1773, aged about 60 years.
Tho' born in the land of slavery,
He was born free.
Tho' he lived in a land of liberty,
He lived a slave.
Till by his honest, tho' stolen labors,
He acquired the source of slavery,
Which gave him his freedom;
Tho' not long before
Death, the grand tyrant,
Gave him his final emancipation,
And set him on a footing with kings.
Tho' a slave to vice,
He practiced those virtues
Without which kings are but slaves.

# The Wayside and the Underground Railroad

Here I am at a plaque that describes the history of The Wayside. It was owned by the Alcott family before it was owned by Nathaniel Hawthorne. This plaque tells the important story that the home of some of America's most famous authors also was a secret hiding place for slaves who were trying to escape using the Underground Railroad. The Alcotts were against slavery and wrote about their strong feelings. But this shows that they walked the walk, too.

# Casey's Home

Here I am standing on the location of a freed Concord slave's home. His name was Casey. After he was freed, he fought in the Revolutionary War. I am all dressed up because I have just come from an opportunity to hear President Obama speak, and I actually got a chance to shake his hand as he looked right at me and said hello. I can barely remember what he said to me because I was in starstruck mode! Barack Obama is the first African American President to serve in the United States. Things have changed a lot since 1775 and 1865!

# President Obama, Governor Patrick, and David Maguire!

Here I am at Barack Obama's speech. He is at the podium, and Governor Deval Patrick is behind him on the stage. Mr. Patrick is the first African American governor of Massachusetts. More and more people of color are holding important positions in government. This shows that Obama and Patrick are not just exceptions. They are the beginning of a trend that blurs racial lines in this country. The Alcotts, Emersons, and Thoreaus would be very happy!

# Thoreau's Path: Named for Slave — Brister Freeman

Here I am at the beginning of Thoreau's path on Brister's Hill, named after another slave of Concord, Brister Freeman. This path leads into Walden Woods. Walden Woods is a famous place where Henry David Thoreau spent two years of his life recording his environment and thinking about the important issues of his day. He was considered an eccentric man, but I think he might have been a man who was ahead of his time and who stood up for what he believed in. He wrote his ideas and became one of America's most famous authors and he took political stands that put him in jail.

# Stone Circle in Walden Woods

Here I am back at the Stone Circle in Walden Woods next to a quote by Martin Luther King Jr., a descendent of slaves who connected his approach to fighting injustice to Henry David Thoreau. The quote is, "A freedom ride into Mississippi, a peaceful protest in Athens, Georgia, are outgrowths of Thoreau's insistence that evil must be resisted and that no moral man can patiently adjust to injustice." King, a social activist for a non-violent struggle for civil rights in the 20th Century, appreciated Thoreau's strong beliefs and principles.

# Civil War Monument

Here I am in front of the Civil War monument, which lists Concord residents who died during the war. An issue is being debated right now about adding the name of the only black Concord resident who enlisted as a Union soldier and never returned home. George Washington Dugan responded to an ad in the *Boston Journal* asking "men of African American descent" to enlist. He left his farm and family to serve his country and was reported as fighting valiantly at Fort Wagner in South Carolina where many died and were tossed in a mass grave. He is officially defined as "Never Accounted For," but people are arguing that he should be treated as a Missing In Action soldier who was killed and added to this monument.

# Part V:

## The Literary Giants of Concord

# The Orchard House:
# Home of the Alcotts

Here I am standing in front of the Orchard House, the home of the Alcotts and the place where Louisa May wrote *Little Women* in only three months in 1868. It is hard for me to imagine that she did not have the right to vote! The Alcotts are a big part of my life because I attended elementary school at the Alcott School, named after Bronson.

# Entrance to the Orchard House

Here I am at the entrance to the Alcott home, a National Historic Landmark. We walked through the inside of the house and could see where the Alcott sisters wrote on the walls because they couldn't afford paper, where they planned and put on their plays, and where Louisa wrote *Little Women.*

# Bronson Alcott's School of Philosophy

Here I am at Bronson Alcott's School of Philosophy, where he first gathered many of the famous Concord philosophers, including Emerson and Thoreau, to discuss philosophical issues. These men eventually founded the Transcendental Movement, which was a literary movement focused on the wonders and the beauty of nature. Anti-slavery, women's rights, and environmentalism began with the philosophies of this movement. *Walden* is one of the most famous books written in the Transcendental tradition. Famous authors such as Walt Whitman and Emily Dickinson talk about how much they were influenced by the writings of the Transcendentalists.

# The Wayside:
# Nathaniel Hawthorne's Home

Here I am next to The Wayside, which, as I mentioned earlier, was once the home of the Alcotts and later the only home that Nathaniel Hawthorne ever owned. Hawthorne did a lot of his writing in the room up on the third floor overlooking the meadows across Battle Road. This home was later owned by Margaret Sidney, who wrote *Five Little Peppers and How They Grew*, a famous children's book of the nineteenth century.

Also, though Louisa wrote *Little Women* in the Orchard House, she and her family actually lived much of the novel here at the Wayside, also known then as Hillside.

And I want to add that I have lived here, too, on a piece of land that was once part of the Wayside and owned back then (at different times) by both the Alcotts and the Hawthornes.

# Renovating the Wayside

Here I am at the Wayside, where my father and I both got a private tour of the Hawthorne home from a Minuteman National Historical Park ranger. We noticed some exterior (paint peeling, rotted wood) as well as some interior damage to the house. It was sad to recall that day that the Wayside had fallen into such disrepair due to lack of funding. So we pointed out what we saw to the ranger.

Next thing we knew, a rehabilitation project had been set in motion that ultimately restored the house to its historical glory. As only a couple weeks had passed since our visit, I assumed we must have had some influence on that ... it felt like too much of a coincidence!

# The Old Manse:
# A National Historic Landmark

Here I am standing beside the description of the Old Manse, another Historic Landmark, which has many connections to both the Revolutionary and the literary periods of Concord.

# Ralph Waldo Emerson's Home

Here I am standing at the entrance of the home that Ralph Waldo Emerson occupied for 50 years. Emerson was probably Concord's most famous citizen, and we can trace his family back to the earliest history of Concord. His study was moved exactly as it was on the day he died to the Concord Museum where one of the lamps ("One if by land, two if by sea") from the Old North Church is also displayed.

# The 1716 Thoreau Room: Colonial Inn

The Thoreau Room in the Colonial Inn is part of the original home. The picture on the wall is of Henry David Thoreau, but it was Thoreau's grandfather who actually lived here. Right outside the window is Monument Hall, where Ralph Waldo Emerson possibly worked for many years.

# Ralph Waldo Emerson's Office in Concord Center

Here I am standing directly across from the Colonial Inn on the road to the Old North Bridge. I am in front of a building where some historians believe Emerson kept an office, and wrote many of his books, poetry and essays. Some say yes, others say no.

I sometimes wish there was such a thing as time travel so we could confirm some of history's mysteries and unanswered questions.

# Thoreau's Cabin on Walden Pond

Here I am standing with Henry David Thoreau in front of a replica of his cabin on Walden Pond. Thoreau lived on the shores of Walden Pond so that he could get close to nature. His lifestyle was very simple and his attention to the details of nature was great.

# Henry David and David at Thoreau's Cabin

Here I am mimicking Thoreau's speaking position. It reminds me of the story about Thoreau when he was in jail for protesting the Mexican War. While Thoreau was imprisoned, his friend Ralph Waldo Emerson visited him. Upon seeing him locked up, Emerson asked, "Henry, what are you doing in there?" Thoreau replied, "Waldo, what are you doing out there?" Thoreau was a passionate opponent of slavery, war, and injustice and, as I pointed out earlier in this book, inspired Martin Luther King Jr. in the Civil Rights movement.

# Henry David Thoreau's Birthplace

Here I am standing in front of Henry David Thoreau's birthplace, right near where my mom and dad work. This house was almost falling down until about a year ago when citizens in our town decided to renovate this important landmark. Many people put in a lot of hours of work to completely redo the building from the inside out!

# Part VI:

## Graves of Famous Concordians

# Louisa May Alcott's Grave

Here I am at the gravesite of Louisa May Alcott, who, as you can see from the symbol, served in the Civil War. This is more evidence that she believed in freeing slaves. Her health failed while she was working in hospitals as a nurse during the war and she never really recovered.

# Thoreau's Grave in Sleepy Hollow Cemetery

Here I am kneeling next to the simple gravestone of Henry David Thoreau in Sleepy Hollow Cemetery on Authors Ridge. Thoreau believed in simple living, so his gravestone reflects his philosophy about material things. Henry David Thoreau championed civil rights and the environment. He fought against slavery and war. Unfortunately, he died of tuberculosis at the young age of 44. How much more could he have influenced our culture if he had been able to live longer?

# Nathaniel Hawthorne's Grave

Here I am next to the grave of Nathaniel Hawthorne, possibly America's greatest author. For example, he wrote *The Scarlett Letter* and *The House of the Seven Gables*. Herman Melville dedicated his famous novel *Moby Dick* to Nathaniel Hawthorne because he admired his work so much. My family owns a summer home on Sebago Lake in Maine. Coincidently, Nathaniel Hawthorne was born and brought up in a home on Sebago Lake. Also, he attended Bowdoin College where he was old college friends with Franklin Pierce, a future president of the United States. The gravestone of poet Ellery Channing is in the background.

# Ralph Waldo Emerson's Gravestone

Here I am at the grave of Concord's most important citizen, Ralph Waldo Emerson. He lived for 78 years, was a Harvard student, wrote poetry and philosophy, and led the Transcendental Movement.

# Ephraim Wales Bull's Grave: Sleepy Hollow Cemetery

Here I am at the grave of Ephraim Wales Bull, who cultivated the Concord Grape. His gravestone is located in Sleepy Hollow Cemetery, just below Authors Ridge.

# Part VII:

## The Concord Grape

# Grapevine Cottage

Here I am at the Grapevine Cottage — the house of Ephraim Wales Bull. The invention of the Concord Grape by creating a hybrid shows that the farmers of Concord were entrepreneurial. The original Concord Grape was planted on this property and Concord grape juice and Concord jelly are still famous today.

# Concord Grape

Here I am on the spot where the original grapevine lives on in Concord, still yielding Concord grapes every year! This is a popular tourist site because people find it hard to believe that the original vine is still alive and producing grapes.

# Part VIII:

## Walden Woods
## Thoreau and the Environment

# Thoreau's Cairn:
# Thoreau's Path in Walden Woods

Here I am placing a stone with my initials on it on a second "Thoreau's Cairn." A cairn is a memorial pile of stones and these stones can come from all over the world. It is an interesting way to think about community. People are all honoring someone they admire by putting their chosen stone on the pile. The first cairn is at Walden Pond near his cabin. You can see the Stone Circle in the background, where there are quotes about the environment and about Thoreau from many famous people.

# The Stone Circle in Walden Woods

Here I am sitting on the stone marked "David" on the Stone Circle in Walden Woods. The adjacent two stones are marked "Henry" and "Thoreau." Interestingly, Henry's name at birth was David Henry Thoreau but in his adult life, for some reason even scholars do not understand, he switched his first and second name to the order we have come to know: Henry David Thoreau.

Thousands of years from now this circle will still be here in memory of Henry David Thoreau's work. I was a radio disc jockey at Lasell College and I often played songs by Eagles. Their lead singer, Don Henley, is the person who helped finance the preservation of Walden Woods.

# Thoreau's Memorial Stone in Walden Woods

Here I am sitting on Thoreau's stone containing his famous quote, "What a miracle of nature it would be if we could for a moment view the world through another's eyes." This is an example of a Transcendentalist's point of view.

our task in our time and in our generation,
to hand down undiminished to those who come after us
as was handed down to us by those who went before,
the natural wealth and beauty which is ours.
To do this will require constant attention and vigilance—
sustained vigor and imagination.

JOHN F. KENNEDY

# John F. Kennedy's Quote at the Stone Circle

Here I am next to President John F. Kennedy's quote about preserving nature for future generations. My youngest sister, Terri, was born just hours before JFK was killed, and my oldest brother is named John Kennedy Maguire. At one time my parents lived in the building in Boston that was JFK's voting address as President. Today, President Kennedy's wisdom is literally carved in stone:

> Thus it is our task in our time and in our generation, to hand down undiminished to those who come after us, as was handed down to us by those who went before, the natural wealth and beauty which is ours. To do this will require constant attention and vigilance — sustained vigor and imagination.

## Dr. Seuss and *The Lorax*
## Walden Woods

Here I am next to the Walden Woods memorial stone containing a poem by Dr. Seuss about why it is important for every individual to do his or her part to protect the environment. An excerpt says,

> "Unless someone like you cares a whole awful lot,
> Nothing is going to get better…
> It's not!"

# David Cox Maguire Walking in Walden Woods

Here I am walking with my dog, Red, in beautiful and peaceful Concord woods, thinking about my life in this town, the great people who have lived here, and the events that have shaped world history. Thoreau wrote about the value and the pleasure of walking in nature.

# Conclusion

# Conclusion

Over the years I have come to Walden Woods often with my parents and our dogs. I hope to come here in the future with my family and to show my children and grandchildren the natural beauty of the place that Henry David Thoreau so loved. I also have visited the many historical sites around Concord, learning about how the authors have written and how the pastors have preached about the political issues of the day and how they have persuaded people's opinions on the issues.

I have learned that cultures change slowly, even when they use bold language about change. Slavery did not disappear when people cried out for freedom and women did not get the right to vote when a democratic government was being formed. But writers and political activists and regular citizens who keep pushing for change help our society become better over time.

So *Here I Am* is a product of my experiences in a town that was the center of memorable historical events and influential people.

I end with a quote from Professor Dennis Frey, which is true of what I learned from CONCORD CONNECTIONS: "Completing this project has enhanced my understanding of how history is about people, places, environments, and monuments — but also about abstract thoughts and concepts. Furthermore, we as individuals make that complex history alive."

# Acknowledgments

# Acknowledgments

My dad for his encouragement throughout the project.  He was involved in every aspect, stimulating ideas, managing photo shoots, and helping with the research.

My mom for her help when I first did this project in college and for her review of this manuscript at key points along the way.

My brother, Matt, for taking photos for this book and for his ability to see things through his lens that many of us miss.

Dr. Dennis Frey, Jr., at Lasell College, for helping me to frame the project when I was a student.

Rick Frese, whose research on Concord history, particularly the Civil War, was really valuable to this book.

Ken Lizotte, who welcomed my idea for a book and made it all possible as the publisher.

Cindy Murphy, who has helped with all of the graphic design, making the pictures and words work together.

Elena Petricone, who has been a helpful part of Ken's team and has taken care of a lot of the details for getting a book ready to publish.

My best friend, Jimmy Hall, for keeping me warm throughout the book by gifting me his jacket. It makes an appearance in many of the photos.

And my beloved dog, Red, who has kept me company as I have worked on this book.

# About the Author

David Maguire

# About the Author

Raised in historic Concord, Massachusetts, David Maguire was born with cerebral palsy and language disabilities. His parents were told by his doctors that he would likely never walk, talk, or attend regular schools. Yet David's indomitable spirit resulted in such miracles as graduating from Concord-Carlisle High School and earning a B.A. in Education, Music and Humanities from Lasell College. Also, according to his dad, he has developed into "one of the finest, kindest young men I have ever known."

Made in the USA
Middletown, DE
05 December 2017